I'M NOT UPSIDE DOWN,
I'M DOWNSIDE UP

of related interest

**The PDA Paradox**
The Highs and Lows of My Life on a Little-Known
Part of the Autism Spectrum
Harry Thompson
Foreword by Felicity Evans
ISBN 978 1 78592 675 4
eISBN 978 1 78592 677 8

**Me and My PDA**
A Guide to Pathological Demand Avoidance
for Young People
Glòria Durà-Vilà and Tamar Levi
ISBN 978 1 78592 465 1
eISBN 978 1 78450 849 4

**Are You Feeling Cold, Yuki?**
A Story to Help Build Interoception and Internal Body
Awareness for Children with Special Needs, Including
Those with ASD, PDA, SPD, ADHD and DCD
K.I. Al-Ghani
Illustrated by Haitham Al-Ghani
ISBN 978 1 78775 692 2
eISBN 978 1 78775 691 5

**Can I Tell You about Pathological Demand
Avoidance Syndrome?**
A Guide for Friends, Family and Professionals
Ruth Fidler and Phil Christie
Illustrated by Jonathon Powell
ISBN 978 1 84905 513 0
eISBN 978 0 85700 929 6

**Pandas on PDA**
A Children's Introduction to Pathological
Demand Avoidance
Glòria Durà-Vilà
Illustrated by Rebecca Tatternorth
ISBN 978 1 83997 006 1
eISBN 978 1 83997 007 8

# I'M NOT UPSIDE DOWN, I'M DOWNSIDE UP

## Not a Boring Book About PDA

Harry Thompson and
Danielle Jata-Hall

Illustrated by Mollie Sherwin

**Jessica Kingsley Publishers**
London and Philadelphia

First published in Great Britain in 2022 by Jessica Kingsley Publishers
An imprint of Hodder & Stoughton Ltd
An Hachette Company

1

A CIP catalogue record for this title is available from the British Library and the Library of Congress

ISBN 978 1 83997 117 4
eISBN 978 1 83997 118 1

Printed and bound in Great Britain by TJ Books Ltd

Jessica Kingsley Publishers' policy is to use papers that are natural, renewable and recyclable products and made from wood grown in sustainable forests. The logging and manufacturing processes are expected to conform to the environmental regulations of the country of origin.

Jessica Kingsley Publishers
Carmelite House,
50 Victoria Embankment,
London, EC4Y 0DZ, UK

www.jkp.com

# CONTENTS

# THIS WILL DO – I HAVE TO START SOMEWHERE!

Oh, hi there. I bet you are looking for the usual boring bits. Well, you won't find them here! You are in a PDA world now, which is like the real world but where everything is turned upside down. If you want a technical explanation then you had better head to the back of the book because for now, if you don't mind, I am going to let you know how it is experienced from the inside.

CHAPTER 1

# THE MOON IS MY SUN

**P**eople see the sun and they think it's a new day. I see the moon and think that **this** is a much better time for the day to begin. Can you see the bed? Have you noticed that I'm not in it? Oh, you weren't expecting me to be in it, were you? I hope not – because that wouldn't exactly stop the bed from being empty now, would it?

In fact, if you **were** expecting me to be snuggled up under the duvet, I would have stepped outside into the cold and laid myself down on the hard concrete, and even though I would be extremely uncomfortable, I would still be happy knowing that I was doing the **exact** opposite of what you'd be expecting me to do.

I would cleverly trick you into thinking that all this time we have been getting it wrong: beds are not just for sleeping in. In fact, I know way funner things to do with a bed, like using it as a trampoline to practise my somersaults or using it as a storage space for my bogies, and even better than that: using it as a giant piece of chewing gum (my dad hates it when I do this, which makes me want to do it even more)!

You see, I can be very forceful with my points, especially when I get into what Mummy calls my 'tsunami' mood. I think if my teacher were to give me homework where I had to explain how sleeping in beds would be the most pointless thing ever then maybe they would find I would be willing to do it for once. And that really is saying something – because I never, EVER, do stupid, boring homework. I would go on about it all day and night until there isn't a person on this earth who hasn't either got rid of their bed or put it to better use.

Do you get the picture now? I will not, under any circumstances, be anywhere near that stupid bed – at least not for sleeping. I mean, do you think cave people slept in a bed? And why doesn't anyone consider the bed's feelings in all this? Doesn't the bed have any say at all? I just want humans to see that they have actually been unkind to beds for years, as, night after night, they lie on top of their poor foamy victims. Beds have rights too, you know!

So that's what happens when people expect me to do normal things like a normal little girl, even on the smallest of scales; the slightest expectation makes me bristle.

Perhaps you are wondering where I am? Well, now you know that the bed is out of the question, I encourage you to have another look.

Yes, that's right, and no, your eyes are not deceiving you: I am upside down in the dog's bed. Do you want to know something else? I don't even own a dog. This is my bed that I sleep in...well... most nights, let's say. Upside down, of course. And by night I mean very late at night – in other words, very early in the morning.

Mummy tells me I don't get enough sleep. And I always say to her that I don't like the thought of missing out. What if something big happens and I'm not there to see it? And what if the world decides to play tricks on me when I'm not looking?

I like being upside down – it's the only way I can sleep. I think it might even be good for me. It sends all the blood to my brain, after all, and having a healthy brain is important to me – because when I am told what to do by people, my brain is my trustiest weapon. When I am told what to do, it's like I am being attacked. My heart starts to race, and I have to find a way to escape the danger. The excuses my brain can quickly come up with often save my life.

**I may look upside down, but to me, the world makes more sense from this angle. In fact, I prefer to see myself as downside up.**

# CHAPTER 2

# FREEDOM IS ME

When I wake up Mummy always says good morning to Daddy and then good morning to my brother, but I hate it when she says good morning to me. I usually shout at her but sometimes she still won't get it. And if she doesn't listen then I step the game up and I throw whatever I can get my hands on.

Do you think I'm being unfair? Well, when I throw something hard at Mummy then it's like when she says good morning to me; it's like she's throwing something hard hitting me in the heart. It's like someone is barging into my world unannounced and uninvited. I tell her all the time that it makes me angry when she tells me my morning should be good, but she never listens.

Besides, my mornings are **never** good anyway, and I wish Mummy wasn't so blind to that.

Mummy says that it is time for school now and I tell her that I should be free! I don't move even though I wish I could. I see other children going to school and it looks like fun, but when I get there it doesn't feel right – my heart still feels empty. I don't understand the other children and they don't understand me. They want the real me to disappear. It's like when I'm there I'm being forced to be a different person.

**Sometimes living in the real world feels like I'm a hamster who has been thrown at a flying flock of birds and I'm expected to fly along with them and then, when I'm in mid-air and I start to fall, I realize I don't have any wings.**

Why is school the only option? I'm designed to do other things. Without freedom I don't want to live. I am freedom, freedom is me. If you remove the freedom there is nothing left of me. I will do anything it takes to learn about the things I'm interested in.

16

I know that we are going to be late, but I haven't even packed my school bag yet. You think I mean all of my things like books, pencils and stuff? No, I put in my bag all my accessories like hairbrushes, bows, clips, dummies and all of my favourite pieces of jewellery. It's far more fun to dress up my friends and give them a makeover, then I feel more able to play with them.

I like playing with people and seeing how they react – I think of them as my living toys. Most people my age play with Lego® or slime but I prefer to make people my toys.

Imagine if your toys suddenly came to life and could attack you; it would be pretty scary. That's how I feel when I can't control people and their every move. Toys are boring; toys are too well behaved. They do everything I tell them. Sometimes I need more of a challenge.

Mummy has a helper called Jenny who comes after school on Mondays (or as I like to say, 'Jennydays') and that's when I get to have the most fun. I stop her at the front door and tell her

she can't move past the welcome mat until she
has changed into the clothes I tell her to wear.
She lets me design her hair and be decorated
in the jewellery I make; the best bit is when I tell
her that her new name is Jessica. I always tell her
that it's my house and I get to make the rules.
Even though Jenny is ancient I consider her my
best friend – perhaps my only real friend.

Sometimes when I know my time with Jenny is coming to an end I start to panic, and I try to distract her so that she doesn't even think about leaving. When she looks at the clock to say we only have five minutes left I quickly run to take the batteries out of the clock. One time she noticed that the hand hadn't moved and asked if the clock was broken but I told her, "No Jenny, you're broken, perhaps you need to stay a little longer and rest."

It didn't work for long. Jenny got up to get her things together so I quickly ran to hide her car keys whilst she wasn't looking. Jenny asked me where her car keys were and I replied, "Car keys? What on earth are car keys? You do realize cars haven't even been invented yet – we are living in the 1800s!"

"Ariana," Jenny softly replied, "I have to get to my next appointment. You know that little boy who is younger than you, who you ask about sometimes? Imagine how upset he will be if I don't get to see him today."

"Don't worry about your car keys – I've disposed of them for you. You can't travel by car, Jessica, you're far too elegant for that. Luckily for you, there is one good way to get around here in the 1800s."

"And what's that?" asked Jenny.

"On horseback, of course!" I said, in an excited way.

Jenny was looking a little irritated by this point, but she couldn't help but smile. "And where am I going to find a horse?" I then dropped to all fours, galloped around the room and neighed. I hoped that this way, if Jenny wasn't able to stay, then I could go with her.

I never want good things to come to an end and the times I spend with Jenny are my happiest times because she accepts me for who I am and never judges me. When Jenny has to go it means I have to go back to feeling lonely and lost again.

# CHAPTER 3

# A TRIP TO
# THE SEWER

I suddenly could hear Mummy calling Mrs Fowell
to say that she couldn't get me ready for school
again today and I could hear Mummy crying. I
wanted to go to school but just couldn't. I hate
it when people want me to do something but for
some reason I just can't. The more they try to
make me the worse it gets. It's in those moments
that I don't want to be me any more.

Mummy comes back into my bedroom to tell
me she has spoken to my school, and she is
disappointed in me. I look away to my pet rats and
remember the time that I locked Jenny out of the
house and waited to see if she would get angry.

She didn't even react and for some reason I didn't feel the need to do it any more. I don't get that upset when she is around – she has that 'thing' that makes me feel calm – just like my rats.

I can see the words coming out of my mummy's mouth but I can't hear them, and I don't want to either. I want to think about my rats, and I always like remembering the first day we met and the reason I chose pet rats in the first place.

Daddy asked me, "What pet would you like?" and I replied,

"A lion."

"We can't have a lion as a pet," said Daddy.

"Well I'll just steal one from the zoo then, and if people catch me the lion can eat them," I corrected him.

"Can't you choose a normal pet like a cat or a dog?" he asked.

"No!" I shouted and thought about it more. "What's your least favourite animal?" I enquired.

"Well, I don't like rats very much," said Daddy.

"Then I **want** a rat! Actually, two rats. You can't have just one rat, they are far too social for that. Let's get a pair of rats and we **must** get them from the sewer," I demanded.

After waiting around with my face down a drain for twenty minutes before I got bored, Daddy took me to the pet shop, but I would not go in until he would agree that we called it the sewer. I watched the brother rats in the cage. I wanted to be the rats – safe and away from the dangerous and confusing world.

I gave the rats some food and they washed themselves afterwards. I was fixated on the rats and nothing else mattered in the world as I knew these rats were supposed to be my pets. My rats don't realize how much they offer me back in return. This is the type of friendship that I can't seem to find in the outside world.

I love my rats with all my heart, but sometimes I do get a kick out of teasing them like I do people. One time, I held a bit of food in my hand near the cage just a little out of their reach. One of them perked up and scurried over towards me. I watched as his eyes lit up and he pressed his face against the cage with his sniffing nose jutting out of the gap, longing for the food that was in my hand. All of a sudden, I stopped what I was doing and realized: 1. how cruel I was being, and 2. how much I related to my rat's situation. I am also a rat trapped in a cage. In my life, the only things that could possibly work for me are beyond my reach. The only things that are available to me, within my cage, are poisonous.

For the second time Mummy comes into my bedroom uninvited, and I say to her, "Mummy, we have spoken about this. You do know this is breaking and entering?"

"We don't have time for games. You're already late for school," Mummy groaned.

"Hmm, what's more important, me or school?" I enquired.

"Darling, we don't have time for..."

"Answer, or I'm never doing anything for you ever again," I demanded. "Never. Ever!"

Mummy sighed and then explained, "Well you need to go to school otherwise you'll never get a good education. And if you don't get an education then you'll never get a decent job."

"I don't feel like I need a teacher. If I wanted one I'd ask you for one. I teach myself things when I'm ready. School doesn't teach me in the way my brain can learn. I'll never be successful at school anyway – because school teaches me that it's not okay to be me!"

I stopped and thought for a moment, and then my anger turned into fear. "I'm trapped in school, then I'm trapped in a job – life is like one big prison sentence! What's the point in that?" Mummy doesn't see what is safe for me; she just wants me to be in the danger zone. "You hate me. I thought you loved me."

"Why do you make our lives so difficult? You're only supposed to be getting ready for school. All I want you to do is put your uniform on – this isn't rocket science!"

"Rocket science – wow! I'd love to do that! Then I could design my own rocket and I'd fly to Mars, and I'd start my own colony full of children just like me. It'd be great. I could make my own rules, and everything would be fair and play would be more important than work."

"Enough of your nonsense, just put your uniform on now!"

"You put the uniform on...you stupid idiot!" I hate the fact that I have to resort to this sometimes, but I'm left with no other choice because she won't get it through her thick skull.

"You are so rude. What have I done to deserve this?" cried Mummy.

At that point, I had to act fast because Mummy wasn't getting the picture, so I picked up the closest thing to me I could find which was this big bag. I had to throw it at Mummy. It was super heavy, but when I'm angry I don't realize how

strong I can be. Mummy flung up her hand to protect herself, and as the bag ripped I saw rat nuggets spill all over the floor. I then realized that what I had used as a weapon was my rats' food. And that's when the true horror set in.

I felt everything inside of me melt as though it was making space for the biggest amount of sadness and worry I had ever felt in my life. The first thing I did was utter "no" so quietly that even I couldn't hear it. This was followed by a series of

"no"s, getting louder and louder as my anxiety grew stronger. I didn't feel like me any more. I was taken over by something horrible and scary. I was so hot. I couldn't breathe. I fell onto the floor and thrashed around. The tears which were streaming down my face and into my mouth were like I was being force-fed sea water.

"KILL ME!" I barked.

"Ariana, please, you're scaring me. What is wrong? How can I help?"

"I am worthless. I am stupid. I don't deserve to live!"

"Of course you do! Why say that? I will be able to help more if I know what the problem is."

"Thanks to me, my rats will now starve!" I then crawled over to Mummy and tightly embraced her legs. "Mummy, please can we go and get some more food, right now. Please." Mummy crouched down to my level and became a bit more sympathetic.

"Hey, Ariana. This problem can be easily fixed. Whilst you are at school, I will go and pick some food up, and it will be here ready for when you get back."

"NO! I have to come too. I need to know that you've bought food for the rats because I can't trust you." I stood up and started frantically putting my uniform on. "I promise you, Mummy," I declared as I stuck out my pinky finger towards her, which she grabbed hesitantly with hers. "Once I have proof that you have bought the right food for my rats, I will go to school straight after. Deal?"

I pulled Mummy by the arm who barely had time to process what was going on, and before she knew it we were in the car and on the way to the pet shop, or the sewer as I like to call it.

CHAPTER 4

# A CHILD WITH A MAN'S FACE

**M**ummy parked the car in a five-storey car park. I don't like car parks because they are dark, damp and scary. But I love the parallel white lines that separate the pedestrian area from the road. I like to walk along the white lines and pretend that I am walking along a narrow plank of wood, thousands of feet in the air. I have to pigeon step along the white line, very carefully, otherwise I will plummet to my death.

I get so fixated when I'm doing this. I am such a perfectionist. One foot after another, and if I so much as touch the black tarmac with my shoe, I lose and have to start all over again. This can drive Mummy mad when we're meant to be going somewhere. But I just can't help it. Walking along the white lines is so satisfying, I sometimes forget what I'm doing.

On that note, what am I supposed to be doing right now? Oh, yes, going to the pet shop to get my rat food. I think we have to get the lift downstairs. Wait a minute... The LIFT?! I look over to see Mummy a few yards ahead of me outside the lift about to press the button. "STOP! DON'T YOU DARE PRESS THAT BUTTON!" I jump

off the white line and sprint over to Mummy and practically barge her out the way as I slam the lift button with my palm. Mummy knows I have to be the first one to press the button, and the first one to enter the lift, otherwise I will not, under any circumstance, go inside.

As we went into the lift, it was nice at first because it was just me and Mummy, but then suddenly the lift stopped on the first floor and too many people came flooding in. I hate it when they do that. How dare they come into **my** lift? As the lift shut, I noticed a strange child. "Look!" I yelled. "Look, Mummy. It's a child with a man's face."

Mummy pulled me closer and yanked my jumper. I could tell I was in trouble but I didn't know why.

"Ariana, that was extremely rude! What were you..." Mummy always does this: she goes to tell me off, but then she takes a breath in and changes her voice. "I know it's hard being you."

I saw Mummy turn around to the boy and say in a shaky voice, "I'm terribly sorry."

Then the boy chuckled and said, "No harm done!"
And at that moment I realized he wasn't a boy,
he was a man – a very small man. Then the man
looked at me; he smiled and didn't tell me off, but
said, "It's okay, I'm like you. From down here I can
stay out of everyone's way." This reassured me
but made me feel more guilty at the same time.

As I watched the man leave the lift, I suddenly
wished I had never said those things at all. This
always happens when I comment on something I
see, and it often gets me into trouble. I can never
understand why – people are always taught to
tell the truth, but when I tell the truth it's wrong.
I looked up at Mummy and asked her, "Do you
think I hurt his feelings?"

Mummy replied, "I know you can't help what you
say, but sometimes what we say can hurt people –
even though it might be true."

I sometimes think about that man and wonder if I
made him feel sad. I didn't mean to upset him. If I
saw him now then I'd let him play with my rats.

By the time we got the rat food I was happy to go back to the car again, but the feeling that I did something wrong and upset the man from the lift kept nagging in my head. I kept trying to talk to Mummy about what had happened, but then her phone started bleeping and school popped onto the screen. Mummy tried to answer the phone and I had to do everything in my power to remind Mummy that I was still alive. I saw the window was open and I felt like something inside me looked at my hand and then looked at the window...and my hand threw the phone out of the window.

Mummy swerved the car over to the side of the road and yanked the handbrake up and I instantly threw my hands over my head to protect myself.

I know that look on Mummy's face – that look she gives me after I do something I can't control that always makes her explode with anger.

"I HATE YOU... It's your fault, you made me do it."

When I'm telling Mummy that I hate her I'm actually talking to myself but facing the opposite way, and the reason for this is that I can't bear to look at myself because I hate myself that much, so instead I fire that hatred at Mummy. But I know it's not Mummy's fault and I feel terrible for saying such horrible things to Mummy. It's not...it's just...sigh...it's so hard sometimes. It looks like I think I'm important and Mummy is beneath me, but it's the total opposite.

To make up for what I'd done I trembled as I told Mummy, "I love you."

I wanted to convince Mummy that what had happened needed to happen. I wanted her to see me looking cool and relaxed about it. Inside though, I felt disgusted with myself. Why did I do that? When I see other people do things like that I hate it. So why would I do that? Surely, if I hate that kind of thing so much, but did it anyway, it had to happen, right? Surely I needed to do that... didn't I?

But I don't think it was working, and I was trying to convince myself too. Maybe deep down I was worried that it was my fault.

# CHAPTER 5

# CHANGE IS MY WORST NIGHTMARE

I don't quite know how to describe how misunderstood I feel by everyone and how invisible they make me feel. I try so hard, and people don't acknowledge my efforts. Even when I'm really stressed out and I'm reaching my limit they mistakenly believe that I am **choosing** to behave badly.

I'll never forget the time when one Christmas we had the family over including my dad's sister who is...YUK! Hang on, I need to gather some strength to talk about her. Right, so here's the situation: I am severely allergic to her. It's not so much that I don't like her but that her very existence insults me and makes me ill!

Sometimes I'm so sick of being myself that I try to be somebody else because the moment I am being myself then something bad always happens to me.

I wanted Christmas Day to go well, and I was trying so hard to fit in and be like everyone else so that we could all have a nice day. I was sitting at the dinner table, and I was trying to be normal, but it was like the environment was launching an attack on me.

There was the sound of my auntie's high heels clip-clopping along the wooden floor and the clinking of knives and forks. I could feel the body heat of the human beings seated too close either side of me; I could hear their breathing, their chewing and their swallowing, and it was making me gag. I could feel their arms moving as they were going for another fork full of food.

The nightmare doesn't stop there. There is the burning anxiety of being asked simple and direct questions. I find big talk is better than small talk – if you mention something I am interested in then you can't get me to shut up. But when people ask boring, everyday questions then I feel like I'm a fish tied to an anchor; the conversation is taking place on the surface and I am being pulled down by the weight and I'm struggling to swim to stay afloat.

What I love most about Christmas is when we get to play the blindfold game where we try to stick the red nose back onto Rudolph. I look forward to it from the moment I wake up, even more than opening my presents. I can just about tolerate this dinner knowing at least what is coming next.

"Ooh, after dinner, I thought we could try this out," interrupted my auntie as she launched a glitzy new karaoke portal onto the table. "It's going to be really fun!"

That was the meteorite that impacted what was an already life-endangering situation. At that point it feels like the world is ending and the life is being squeezed out of my body and I am desperately trying to stay in control. If I have any chance of staying alive then we have to stick to the plan. To go against my plan is putting me in danger.

I could not keep up the act any longer. I grabbed my plateful of Christmas dinner and launched it across the living room, almost hitting my daddy on the head as it flew past him.

"Christmas is the worst day of the year!" I screamed, before saying a rude word at the top of my lungs.

Disgusted with my behaviour, my auntie said, "Don't be so rude and selfish! You can't always get what you want! Your parents have made you a lovely meal and you are embarrassing them and making yourself out to be ungrateful. You don't see anyone else throwing a tantrum, do you? Show some respect!"

I had been negated at that point. "No one understands what it's like to be Autistic," I thought. "No one has recognized how hard I've tried prior to this incident. No one is even considering the fact that this behaviour has nothing to do with me being rude but is the result of a panic attack. A panic attack resulting from the plan being changed – a worst nightmare for me.

Why isn't it disrespectful when people expect me to be someone I'm not? Why isn't it rude that people haven't even bothered to understand before judging me? Why is it out of order for me to express my true feelings? Why is it not unacceptable of them to tell me that it's wrong to be myself? Why can't they see how hard I have to try to behave 'normally', that normal is almost impossible for me to achieve? If I do achieve it, I can't keep it up for long until I break. Why are they not grateful that I have put my true self on hold just so they could enjoy their meal? Why are they not appreciative of the fact that I wanted to enjoy the meal as well and tried my hardest not to do anything 'too weird' purely out of respect for them? Why is it always me who has to change when I'm the one who finds being alive the most difficult?"

I bet if you are anything like me, then you too won't enjoy dwelling on the moments when you have been in a big meltdown. I don't like thinking about it or else my inner beast could strike again!

Anyway, back to the story...

# CHAPTER 6
# I'M NOT LATE, THE TEACHER IS

I said to Mummy, "Maybe it's time to go to school now," and Mummy opened her mouth so wide I saw the dangly bit at the back of her throat: *sniff sniff* "Hmm, did you brush your teeth this morning?"

Mummy dropped me off and I wandered over to the part of the playground which my classroom overlooked. I couldn't bring myself to walk through the door so I loitered here until my teacher, Mrs Fowell, saw me and came outside.

"Are you coming in then?" Mrs Fowell snarled.

"Who? I'm not real," I wittily replied.

The teacher malfunctioned and said, "You!"

Mrs Fowell is not exactly known for her sense of humour. She is a stern, stuffy woman, whose coffee breath smells like regurgitated spaghetti bolognese. And, if I'm being picky, she has too much space between her nose and upper lip.

"Oh, sorry, I forgot that you're brain damaged."
The reason I said this is because the part of the
brain where playfulness and imagination live is
missing in normal people. "Once the caretaker
removes the thorns from the doorway, I'll
consider it; it's a bit of a health hazard, you
know!" You could tell I was really getting on Mrs
Fowell's nerves. You might think me cruel and I
suppose I am a bit, but I just can't help myself –
being difficult is one of my favourite pastimes.

Mrs Fowell looked over to the door to find no
thorns. I had never seen anyone look quite so
unimpressed in all my life.

"Mrs Fowell? That must mean there's a **Mr** Fowell?
Oh, goodness... Oh, no... Tell him that I am so
sorry he has to put up with you every day!"

"Why are you late?" she said, clearly ignoring me.

"I'm not. YOU are!" And with that, I sprinted inside
the classroom and sat in Mrs Fowell's chair. The
other children looked up at me in disbelief. Mrs
Fowell eventually caught up, and I greeted her

with, "Ah, Mrs Fowell, about time you joined us! Come on in and sit down." I gestured to the empty chair and desk that was usually mine.

The teachers at the school had had just about enough of my shenanigans and thought it was a good idea for me to see an 'educational psychologist', whatever that is. I understand that a psychologist is someone who tries to get inside your mind, but as far as I'm aware, education doesn't have a mind, because it's not a person. But then again, neither am I... Anyway, one day after school (on a day I couldn't even bring myself to go in), Mummy and I went to see Psycho Ed.

# CHAPTER 7
# PSYCHO ED

The first thing I did when I arrived at Psycho Ed's office was to lay on the floor and kick my legs into the air.

"Oh, and I suppose you are a rabbit?" enquired Psycho Ed (she did tell me her name, but I prefer Psycho Ed and I can't remember what her name is anyway).

"Of course I'm not!" I declared. "I don't like rabbits; they are far too fluffy! Now rats, rats are definitely more endearing. I am a rat who happens to enjoy kicking. Get it right!"

"Mummy tells me that you refuse to get ready for school. Do you want to tell me about what happened this morning?" she asked softly.

"Crispies!" I blurted. "What is this, an interrogation?"

"Rice crispies? Oh, is that what you had for breakfast?" Psycho Ed responded, ever hopeful for some kind of progress.

"No! Ready salted crispies! I want them now!" I demanded.

"What happened this morning?" Psycho Ed pried, trying her hardest to ignore me.

"I ate crisps..." I muttered smilingly.

"And before that?"

"I had a dream that I ate a monster eyeball."

"Well, what happened before you ate the monster eyeball?"

"My mummy took me in the car to come here."

"And why did Mummy bring you here?"

I ran out of the room, but Mummy was still in there. I threw some things outside, but she still didn't come out. I had no choice but to go back into the room. But if I was to go back into the room, things would be a little different!

"Okay, I'm ready to engage properly now," I said like a good, sweet little girl as I pointed to a book on the shelf that was a little out of my reach. "That looks like a lovely story. Would you be so kind as to hand it to me, please?"

For no good reason Mummy went to stand up as if I had asked her. "Excuse me, don't be so rude, that's not your bookshelf! I asked Psycho Ed... Edwina." (I thought it would sound more polite if I gave her an actual girl's name.) Psycho Edwina smirked at me before getting up to fetch me the book from the shelf and the moment her bottom was in the air, I darted towards her chair and sat on it.

"So, did you do a fart at work today? And where did you do your poo, at home or work? Was it green?!" I asked with a clever and tactical subject change.

"I am one to use the toilet at home," Psycho Edwina surrendered.

"What did you eat for breakfast? Why do you have that watch? Where did you get those red veins in your eyes from?" I had to ask a series of questions because not only did it throw her off balance, but it also distracted me from my painful feelings.

"It must be exhausting," Psycho Edwina said out of the blue, which stopped me in my tracks.

"What is?" I retorted.

"Always running away when you're being chased by those horrible feelings." All I could do was stare. Psycho Edwina's words stung, but what she said was true, and that made me a feel a little better. Nobody had ever reacted to me like that before; I'm used to being told off and I'm used to being judged.

"If I tell you more about how I feel, you're not going to hurt me, are you?" I asked tentatively.

"Of course not," Psycho Edwina reassured. "Here you are safe to talk, and you are safe to be you."

"I remember on my brother's birthday, Mummy got me a card that she wanted me to write for him. I couldn't do it and Mummy got really, REALLY cross. She kept asking me, and I kept saying no, even though inside I was angry with myself and really wanted to do it. She said either write the card or go to your room. And I said that

I will go to the room, even though I didn't really want to, because I was prepared to do ANYTHING instead of writing the card.

I think her anger was actually disguising her sadness, because just before she closed my bedroom door on me, she said, with a tear in her eye and a tremble in her voice, 'I can't believe how horrible you are to people sometimes.' When she left my room, I looked at the photo of my brother and me on my windowsill and I started to cry myself. I felt like the most disgusting person on the planet.

If there's one thing I want people to know, it's that when I'm being difficult I'm not enjoying myself. I feel very guilty knowing that I'm making everyone's life hard, but what people don't realize is that the reason I act like this is because I find life hard too. And sometimes I wonder if I find life harder than other people because I feel like this all the time.

The times after I explode are the hardest because sometimes even though I feel so much regret I can't bring myself to say sorry because that's a demand too. And because I don't say sorry people don't know how bad I feel. I know this sounds strange but when I'm having a meltdown it's like it's not even me who's doing it. Like I'm watching something else take over me and I don't even have the power to stop it.

Sometimes, it feels like I am stuck in a demand prison, and I am not allowed to enjoy a normal, let alone a happy, life."

I paused for a moment, and told the Psycho... ahem...educational psychologist, "I can't hurt any more people. I deserve to be the one who gets hurt. What people don't understand about me is that sometimes, I feel like Beauty and the Beast. They are both me. When the Beast comes out, I just can't stop it. After the Beast has gone, Beauty is there, and she feels very sorry."

At that point I started crying and hugged my mummy tightly – this wasn't me having a meltdown; I knew this was the real me – and I said to my mummy, "I'm sorry for the way that I am sometimes."

Mummy opened her bag and passed me my rabbit and softly said, "You've been very brave opening up today and because of that I feel like I understand you a lot more. How about you, Rabbit and I take a visit to the new ramps at the skatepark and get an ice cream for the journey home?"

"Are you going to have an ice cream too, Mummy?"

"Oh yes, well I can do, that would be nice." I looked down and thought for a moment.

"Could I wee on it?"

Mummy looked at me in disgust for a brief moment and then laughed her head off, then she scooped her arm around me and we shut the door of the psycho room behind us.

# CHAPTER 8
# MY HAPPY PLACE

On the way to the skatepark I asked Mummy, "Are there other things similar to that which I could do?"

"Hmm," Mummy thought. "I suppose there are many different types of therapies such as art therapy, animal therapy..."

"Mummy, what does 'therapy' mean anyway?" I interrupted.

"Well, I suppose it's anything that makes you feel better."

"But why was that the only time I've spoken to an adult and actually felt better?" I remarked. "Besides, she wasn't even a therapist."

I was relieved to get to the skatepark; this is my happy place. I know the course of every ramp and how to jump over every grind rail. I noticed they had built a new ramp, which was a bit annoying. I don't know why they didn't ask for my permission first.

It wasn't very busy that day; I always prefer it when it's quiet. Still, I instantly formed a bond with another child – a little boy around my age. "I've had a really nice day today," I expressed to the boy.

"Okay..." he responded.

"Well, have you?" I continued.

"Yeah, I guess so. Would you like to skate down the new ramp with me?" he asked.

"You're lucky I'm in a good mood because I would have said no. I'm scared of the ramp not because it's big but because it's new." He didn't really understand what I meant but it didn't matter. We smiled at each other as we skated off to the new ramp.

And that's when I realized what therapy actually means. It's not about an adult in an office trying to make you feel better (that never works for me), but rather when you least expect it you share a lovely moment with someone. That's what makes me feel better.

EPILOGUE

# BORING BITS

Okay, so PDA is largely considered to be a profile that fits within the Autistic three-dimensional space; I refuse to call it a spectrum because that's what boring, fart-head doctors call it and Autistic three-dimensional space is the preferred terminology from an Actually Autistic doctor.

Oh, you're probably wondering what being Autistic means. Being Autistic means that I experience the world differently to how other people experience the world...because my brain is different. It's like my senses are heightened or dimmed. When there is too much going on around me and I'm stressed and overwhelmed, the feel of certain textures can calm me down, like when I stroke my rats and when I touch my toy rabbit's label.

But all Autistic people are different: some may really like the sound of the wind rustling in the trees, whilst others may hate it. Likewise, some may really like the smell of petrol, and for others it makes them light-headed. The same applies to tastes and sights. Some might enjoy the strange sensation on your tongue when sticking it to a battery. I, for example, cannot deal with screens going blurry or pixelated when the computer glitches; it makes me feel like I want to puke!

Being Autistic also means my interests are very strong and intense, and I pay close attention to the details that other people might miss. Sometimes when I'm speaking to people it's like we can't quite understand each other, even though we are speaking the same language, because we have different communication styles. They want to have small talk, but I prefer to have big talk. They want to natter on about everyday things, whereas I want to tackle the big questions of life, like for instance – what happened before the big bang? And also, why did we get born with one big toe and four little toes to keep the big one company?

Now let's talk about PDA.

PDA stands for Pathological Demand Avoidance, but I find that such a tongue-twister. I much prefer saying I'm PDA instead, without worrying about what the letters stand for. PDA is not something I have; PDA is what I am. I am free no matter what.

PDA means that there are going to be things that people expect me to do, and even things I want to do myself, that I simply can't do. It's not a case of me **choosing** not to do things; it's as I said before: I **can't**. When people want me to do something, I have a lot of clever and funny excuses that I use to trick them. Sometimes if I'm really anxious and my brain can't come up with something witty, I may end up trying to shock people instead. I feel a sense of calm when other people are confused; it feels like they are really seeing me.

Sometimes I don't know why I'm so driven to avoid. Sometimes I really want to do the thing, but because it's an expectation I have to avoid it as my freedom has to come first every time. Nobody gets to tell me what to do and gets away with it.

When the world leaves me to my own devices I get on with my life. PDA doesn't mean I don't do anything at all; it means I will only do something when it is right and when it is safe.

Avoiding demands isn't all that PDA is. PDA also means that I get fascinated with people in either a loving or hateful way. It is also the reason I can come up with such creative and clever phrases and why I can think in such an out-of-the box kind of way, why I have such a rich fantasy world, why I am a good actor and why I am perfectly me.

Okay, so those are the amazing things about me. But when I'm in the wrong place, being PDA means that I can struggle a great deal, and because of this people end up struggling as a result. I am described as unpredictable and challenging, but what people don't understand is that I, myself, am challenged when I am in a dangerous environment surrounded by people who don't understand me.

I think you get the picture and I'm bored now. If you still don't understand PDA then I really can't help you any more. May I suggest you get a new brain? Perhaps a PDA brain would help!

And don't think you are getting a goodbye from me. You can have my tongue instead.